Genre Realistic Fi

Essential Question
How do your actions affect others?

Rosa's Garden

by Eve Tonkin | illustrated by Abigail Marble

Chapter 1

The Empty Lot

Everyone in Rosa's neighborhood complained about the empty lot. Piled high with trash, old tires, and broken junk, it looked terrible, and in summer—*whew*, it smelled!

What's more, the lot was no longer a safe place to play. The ground was cracked, and kids were always tripping over trash. Rosa remembered how much fun she and her friend Maria used to have playing there. Now it was too dangerous.

Jamal's mom grumbled to Rosa's mom. "I've told Jamal he's not to play there anymore. The problem is that it's much closer than the park."

"Don't get me started!" Rosa's mom replied. "I'm tired of picking up trash over there. I feel humiliated living next to it."

Rosa stood at the window, staring down at the empty lot. Rain seemed to fall like a curtain, separating their place from everywhere else.

Rosa watched the rain make puddles in the lot. It pooled in the old tires and soaked clumps of trash. From above, the lot looked like a giant pot of trash soup.

Then Rosa noticed the flowers in the window boxes outside Mr. Johnson's apartment. The bright pinks and purples of the flowers stood out against the gray color of the day.

"Mr. Johnson's plants are the only nice things out there," Rosa thought. Suddenly inspiration struck.

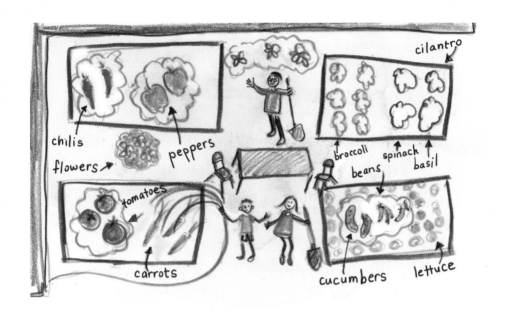

"You know how everyone is always complaining about the vacant lot?" Rosa said that evening. "Well, I've thought of a way to fix it!" She presented her parents and her brother, Diego, with a drawing she had done. "It's my dream for the lot," she explained.

"What a beautiful drawing, Rosa!" her mom exclaimed. "I love the chili plants and the pretty flowers."

"It's really cool," Diego agreed.

"A garden's a fantastic idea, Rosa," her father said. "Let's see if we can make your dream happen."

Chapter 2

Growing Begins

A month later, Rosa's father had some good news. "The city is going to allow us to turn the lot into a community garden," he said. "They're going to clear away the junk this week!"

On Saturday, the neighbors met at the lot, which already looked much better without the junk. First, everyone picked up the remaining trash, and then they began creating garden beds.

"This is hard work!" said Diego's friend David.

"Hard work builds character and self-esteem," Rosa's dad said, launching into his favorite speech. "It helps you to grow as a person, and—"

"The dump truck's arrived!" Diego shouted. The kids ran to watch the truck empty its load of dirt.

Then David's father arrived in a pickup. "The compost is here!" he yelled. "I advise you to work hard—if you don't pull your weight, you'll end up shoveling compost!"

Finally, they began planting. Every family took one garden bed, except Mr. Johnson and Mr. Garcia, who decided to share one.

It was early evening by the time everyone had finished planting. "This looks awesome!" Diego said to Rosa.

"Look out!" yelled David, showering the children with the hose.

Jamal's mom laughed as the kids started to dance in and out of the spray.

Chapter 3

The Missing Vegetables

"Hurry up," Rosa called to Diego, "or we won't be able to check out the garden before school!"

Summer had almost arrived, and the plants were getting taller. The lettuce and other salad greens were growing. Small green tomatoes were appearing, and yellow beans were poking through the green leaves.

Warm sun slanted across the sidewalk as Rosa, Diego, and Maria walked to the garden. "I wonder if anything's ripe yet," Diego said, running ahead.

Suddenly he turned around looking dismayed.

"Our plants are wrecked!"

It was true. Most of the salad greens had been pulled out, and some of the tomato vines had been trampled. Tears filled Rosa's eyes.

"Come on," Maria said. "We'll be late for school. Mr. Johnson or Mr. Garcia will be along soon. They'll tell the others."

Before class, Rosa and Maria told their friends and teacher about their missing vegetables.

"There were pieces of lettuce lying around," said Rosa.

"And broken stalks," added Maria.

"The mess suggests that an animal may have eaten the vegetables," Mrs. Fuller said. "Did you look for tracks?"

Rosa hesitated. "No…but we wouldn't have known what kind of animal left the tracks."

"I can help you there," said Mrs. Fuller. "Let's see if we can find a book on animal tracks at the library today."

When the children arrived at the garden after school, Mr. Johnson and Mr. Garcia were already there. "What if they've cleaned everything up and we can't find any tracks!" Maria said desperately.

"Did you hear about our missing vegetables?" Mr. Garcia called.

"Yes," Rosa replied. "We've brought a book that shows different animal tracks!"

"This is interesting," Mr. Garcia said, looking at the book. "Mr. Johnson and I figured it might be an animal, and then Mr. Johnson discovered some prints behind your tomatoes."

"No doubt about it," said Mr. Johnson, looking at the page. "It's definitely a raccoon!"

"Let's call City Hall and ask them to send out an animal control officer," said Mr. Garcia. "They're accountable for getting rid of unwanted animals."

The next day, people from the building met in Mr. Garcia's apartment.

"I have some good news!" said Mr. Garcia. "The city has received other complaints about raccoons in the area."

"That's hardly good news," Mr. Johnson said jokingly.

"But it is," Mr. Garcia replied, "because the city can give us a fence to keep the raccoons out!"

"We could even build a special gate," suggested Rosa eagerly.

Chapter 4

The Garden in Bloom

A few months later, Rosa was walking to the garden with her mom and some friends for Rosa's birthday party.

When they reached the garden, the girls admired the new fence and its funky gate.

"Our friend Mr. Garcia helped us make it from trash," Maria explained.

"Who made that beautiful sun?" Jolie asked.

"Rosa, of course," Maria replied.

Rosa blushed uncomfortably as a cheer went up from the community gardeners.

As Rosa and Maria showed their friends around the garden, they picked tomatoes. "They taste so good!" exclaimed Kimora.

Diego ran up to them. "Dad says it's time for the piñata."

Everyone had fun hitting the piñata, and after Maria had dealt the final blow, Rosa's mom brought out a huge cake covered with flowers from the garden.

"I'd like to thank you, Rosa," her dad said. "Without your imagination, we wouldn't be in this beautiful garden today!"

Rosa smiled at her friends and neighbors. She realized that one small idea could make a big change if people worked together.

Respond to Reading

Summarize

Use details from *Rosa's Garden* to summarize the story. Your graphic organizer may help you.

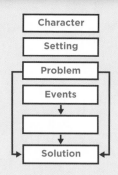

Character

Setting

Problem

Events

↓

↓

Solution

Text Evidence

1. What kind of fiction story is *Rosa's Garden*? How can you tell? GENRE

2. What is the problem with the garden on page 9? PROBLEM AND SOLUTION

3. What does Rosa's mother mean when she says, "Don't get me started!" on page 3? IDIOMS

4. Write about how Rosa and her neighbors solve the problem described on page 9. WRITE ABOUT READING

Compare Texts

Read about how community gardens improve neighborhoods.

FRESH FROM THE CITY

People who live in cities usually buy their fruits and vegetables from supermarkets. However, more and more people are growing their own food. Thousands of empty lots in city neighborhoods have been turned into community gardens.

GROW YOUR OWN FOOD

As Rosa and her friends discovered, a home-grown tomato can taste much better than a store-bought tomato.

The fruits and vegetables you buy from a supermarket are often a few weeks or months old. Chemicals are usually used to help the fruits and vegetables grow.

Fresh vegetables grown in a garden taste delicious.

Community gardens are good for neighborhoods in other ways, too. When an empty lot is turned into a garden, the neighborhood looks better. In addition, gardening gives neighbors a chance to work together.

Saving money is another great reason for starting a community garden. For example, between 2007 and 2010, many people in Cleveland, Ohio, lost their jobs when factories closed down. Some supermarkets also closed, so people couldn't buy fresh food.

That's when the city began helping people turn empty lots into community gardens. City farming saved people in Cleveland money and helped them have fresh fruits and vegetables to eat.

Many community gardens are started by volunteers who want to clean up empty lots in their neighborhoods.

Would you like to grow your own fresh food? Even if you don't have much space, you can still grow food in containers.

MAKING A CONTAINER GARDEN

1. You can make a garden using old tires, plant pots, or bathtubs.

2. Create drainage by putting gravel in the bottom of your container. If you are using a container without holes at the bottom, ask an adult to help you make some holes.

3. Fill your containers two-thirds full with moist, crumbly soil and compost.

4. Dig small holes in the soil, put your plants in, then add more soil around them.

5. Place your containers in a sunny spot. Water your plants regularly.

Make Connections

How does a community garden help a neighborhood? ESSENTIAL QUESTION

What have you learned from *Rosa's Garden* and *Fresh from the City* about the ways people can make a difference in their communities? TEXT TO TEXT

Focus on Literary Elements

Idioms Idioms are words or phrases that have a different meaning from the meaning of the actual words. For example, the idiom *sit on the fence* means that you can't make up your mind about something. To *pull someone's leg* means to play a joke on them or tease them.

Read and Find On page 6 in *Rosa's Garden*, David's father tells everyone to "pull their weight" when they are making the garden. This means he wants everyone to work as hard as they can.

Your Turn

The idiom *piece of cake* means that something is easy to do. *Against the clock* means that you are in a hurry and don't have much time. With a partner, make a list of idioms you know. Talk about what they mean. Write sentences using the idioms from your list. Share what you wrote with another group.